W9-CBP-548

SILVERCHEST

SILVERCHEST

CARL PHILLIPS

FARRAR STRAUS GIROUX

NEW YORK

Farrar, Straus and Giroux
18 West 18th Street, New York 10011

Printed in the United States of America
First edition, 2013

Library of Congress Cataloging-in-Publication Data
Phillips, Carl, 1959–
    Silverchest / Carl Phillips. — 1st ed.
    p. cm.
    ISBN 978-0-374-26121-4 (alk. paper)
    I. Title.

PS3566.H476 S55 2013
811'.54
                                2012034565

Designed by Quemadura

www.fsgbooks.com
www.twitter.com/fsgbooks
www.facebook.com/fsgbooks

1 3 5 7 9 10 8 6 4 2

Like a knife in a melon, Autumn slices Summer.

It will be cold, going back.

TU FU

CONTENTS

★

★

SILVERCHEST

JUST THE WIND FOR A SOUND, SOFTLY

There's a weed whose name I've meant all summer
to find out: in the heat of the day, dangling pods hardly
worth the noticing; in the night, blue flowers . . . It's as if
a side of me that he'd forgotten had forced into the light,
briefly, a side of him that I'd never seen before, and now
I've seen it. It is hard to see anyone who has become
like your own body to you. And now I can't forget.

AND OTHER ANIMALS

Roughly the river, running swift, and silver.
The usual more sluggish business of erosion
to either side of it—this life,

for that one. Green

ambivalence of the trees where the forest shelves:
so the dark deepens. So the dead become earth
and then nothing, things that will never matter
now in the way they used to, for—

yes, they

used to, or so we tell ourselves, pretending grief
is like that. Wishes, rising suddenly up elsewhere,
take their places in a shifting line called *Better wish
again.* Maybe joy really

is a kind of spindrift—

spinning, drifting—on a sea of sorrow, though it
looked like prayer, and it felt like power, them
kneeling before me as if to receive at last their crowns.

SO THE MIND LIKE A
GATE SWINGS OPEN

When it comes to what, eventually, it must come to,
don't forget to say to yourself *Has it come to this again
already?* Look a little lost, maybe,

                         but unsurprised.
Sometimes it feels like being a carousel horse, but
with all the paint gone strange-like, all the wood gone
driftwood, all the horses I've corralled inside me set free,
confused now, because now what? The snow fell like
hope when it's been forsaken, just before the wind shifts—
then the wind shifts, the snow flies upward . . . I love you
means what, exactly? In the end, desire may turn out
to be no different from any other song—

                         sing, and be at
last released from it. Not so long ago as I'd like to think,
I used to get drunk in parking lots with strangers: we'd park,
we'd drink, and—and didn't think what to call it, the rest
that came after, what is a thing like that worth calling: he

took me into his arms? he held me? I know longing's
a lot like despair: both can equal everything you've ever
hoped for, if that's how you want it—sure, I get that. *What's
wrong with me*, I used to ask, but usually too late, and not
meaning it anyway. He touches me, or I touch him, or don't.

THE JETTY

Some are willing to trust any anchor. Some will
choose the ship anyway, no matter how anchorless
and dashed, between the wind and the sea. The sea
the same then as now: more blear than blue, more
blue than silver—processional, seeming to blur
at once increasingly and at random toward and
away from where everything catches fire except
what doesn't. How they fucked him, yes, until
he couldn't, yes, but—couldn't what. The raptor's
wing unfolds, and then folds back. We turn here, but
separately. Did his eyes close. Did he close them.
Look how the jetty shines in the sun, for nothing.

NOW ROUGH, NOW GENTLE

Never mind the parts that came later, with all
the uselessness, as usual, of hindsight: regret's
what it has to be, in the end, in which way it is
like death, any bowl of sliced-fresh-from-the-tree
stolen pears, this body that stirs,

                        or fails to, as I
turn away, meaning *Make it yours*, or *Hold tight*,
or *I begin to think maybe you were right—that
there's nothing, after* . . . though whether or not like
one of those moments just past having woken to
yet another stranger,

                  how the world can seem
to have completely stopped when, finally, it's just
a stillness—who can say? First I envied them,
then I came to love them for it, how the stars each
day become again invisible, while going nowhere.

FLIGHT OF DOVES

I have been the king for whom the loveliest beasts
were slaughtered and turned trophy. I've seen how
brutality becomes merely the rhythm to a kind of
song to sing while bearing the light steadily forward,
the light in panels, in the shape that luck mostly takes

before a life comes true again: the room no different
than I remember leaving it: the snow still falls into it,
on the same man bound naked to a chair, and trembling,
saying *Take me*—meaning what, though, or where?—as
I brush the snow from his hair, as I take him, in my arms.

SURROUNDED AS WE ARE, UNLIT, UNSHADOWED

Squalor of leaves. November. A lone
hornets' nest. Paper wasps. Place where
everything that happens is as who says it will,
because. As in *Why shouldn't we have
come to this, why not*, this far, this
close to
          that below-zero where we almost
forget ourselves, rise at last unastonished
at the wreckery of it, what the wreckage
somedays can seem all along to have
been mostly, making you wonder what fear
is for, what prayer is, if not the first word
and not the last one either, if it changes
nothing of what you are still, black stars,
black
          scars, crossing a field that you've
crossed before, holding on, tight, though

careful, for you must be careful, so easily
torn is the veil diminishment comes
down to as it lifts and falls, see it falling,
now it lifts again, why do we love, at all?

BLUEGRASS

And he told me nowhere was a lake that,
any day now, he'd surely drown in. What's the right
answer to a thing like that?

★

So we just stood there,
the two of us—shaking a bit in the cold,
but pretty still, mostly. Horses in a field of moonlight.

AFTER THE AFTERLIFE

Bones, for sure. Feathers almost the white
of an eagle's undershaftings in its first year.
Any wind, that stirs. Punishment in death
as it is in trembling: how it lifts, descends,
though—like having meant to be kind, yet
failing anyway—it can do no good. After
the afterlife, there's an afterlife. A stand of
cottonwood trees getting ready all over again,
because it's spring, to release their seeds that
only look like cotton; they're not cotton, at all.
What we lose, without thinking to; what we
give, for free. Distinctions that, if they even
did before, now don't matter. Any shadows
that break break randomly across these waters.

FIRST YOU MUST
COVER YOUR FACE

There's a handful of black bees fastened
to the crepe myrtle's shot, all-but-gone-to-seed
flowers. Is it days, really, or only moments ago
that I almost told you everything,
before remembering what that leads
or has led to? How still they are—the bees, I mean,
not the flowers bending and unbending beneath
a rain that's come suddenly and, just as suddenly,
has stopped falling . . . Stillness, not of death,
but intoxication,
sweet coma,
zero-ness of no more wanting,
nothing left to want for, the meadow at last
fills with light, like a bowl,
filled with light, spilling with it, only harder now,
as if more desperate maybe, or just a thing that's brave.

BLACK SWAN ON WATER, IN A LITTLE RAIN

Seen this way,
through that lens where need
and wanting swim at random

toward each other, away again, and
now and then together, he moves less like
a swan—black, or otherwise—than like any

man for whom sex is, or has at last become,
an added sense by which to pass ungently but more
entirely across a life where, in between the silences,

he leaves what little he's got to show for himself
behind him in braids of water, green-to-blue wake of
Please and *Don't hurt me* and *You can see I'm hurt, already.*

MY MEADOW, MY TWILIGHT

Sure, there's a spell the leaves can make, shuddering,
and in their lying suddenly still again—flat, and still,
like time itself when it seems unexpectedly more
available, more to lose therefore, more to love, or
try to . . .

      But to look up from the leaves, remember,
is a choice also, as if up from the shame of it all,
the promiscuity, the seeing-how-nothing-now-will-
save-you, up to the wind-stripped branches shadow-
signing the ground before you the way, lately, all
the branches seem to, or you like to say they do,
which is at least half of the way, isn't it, toward
belief—whatever, in the end, belief

                    is . . . You can
look up, or you can close the eyes entirely, making
some of the world, for a moment, go away, but only
some of it, not the part about hurting others as the one
good answer to being hurt, and not the part that can
at first seem, understandably, a life in ruins, even if—

refusing ruin, because you
                          can refuse—you look
again, down the steep corridor of what's just another
late winter afternoon, dark as night already, dark
the leaves and, darker still, the door that, each night,
you keep meaning to find again, having lost it, you had
only to touch it, just once, and it bloomed wide open . . .

DISTRACTION

He did what I told him to,
which for once I thought shouldn't count

as weakness: he laid his gun on the bureau,
took his own shirt off first, then mine—but then wrapped
the gun up softly inside the both of them, sign
for many things, *Trust me, Close your eyes, Make a wish*,

so that I couldn't decide . . .

                   You know how, when the light
flashes off water, then passes through it, then rubs up against,
it can seem just like the mind in a fix thinking its way
out of a fix, or at least trying to, the way Virgil in his
big poem describes it, and for a moment you think

everything's new that's been known forever—swamp-thistle,
bull-thistle, touch-me-not, red clover?

THE DIFFERENCE BETWEEN POWER AND FORCE

In the east country where I must have lived once,
or how else remember it, the words came falling to
every side of me, words from a life that I'd thought,
if not easy, might at least be possible, though that
was then: *little crown* and *little burst of arrows*

and *ritual, loyalty, they are not the same* . . . I lay
rippling like a field shot through with amethyst
and reason. Then it seemed I myself was the field,
the words fell toward, then into me, each one no
sooner getting understood, than it touched the ground.

DARKNESS IS
AS DARKNESS DOES

All night long, he's been a music almost
too far away to hear, and the man who
thinks he hears something that could maybe
be music: bits of flourish where there can't
or shouldn't be. As when camouflage matters
suddenly less than stillness. *Nothing in this world
like being held*, he says, turning away, meaning

I should hold him . . . I have been to Rome,
I have known the body, I have watched it fall,

and the green, green grass. How the deer re-
unsettled themselves across it, disproportionately
clumsy, for when they ran, there was grace. Then
the dream dog emerging again—hindquarters
first, as if dragging a great heaviness finally free
from the stand of trees that swayed, for a while,
the way bamboo does. Then silver birches.

23

NEON

A boy walks out into a grayish distance, and he never comes back.
Anger confusable with sorrow, sorrow canceling all the anger out . . .
It's the past, and it isn't. It's forever. And it isn't. The way, in hell,
flickering's what they say what's left of the light does—a comfort,
maybe, and maybe not. Sometimes by innocence I think I've meant
the innocence of carnivores, raised in the wild, for whom the killing
is sportless, clean, unmetaphysical—then I'm not so sure. Steeplebush
flourished by some other name, lost now, long before there were
steeples. I think we ruin or we save ourselves. Comes a day when
the god, what at least you've called a god, takes you not from behind,
the usual, but pins you instead, his ass on your chest, his cock in your
face, his mouth twisting open, saying *Lick my balls*, and because you
want to live, in spite of everything, you do what he says, heaven and
earth, some rain, a few stars appearing, harder, the way he tells you to,
then not so hard, a tenderness like no tenderness you've ever shown.

GHOST HOUR

Scattered soot, by which the myth you made for yourself,
before at last becoming the myth, has sometimes been
more easily understandable—but sometimes not—there's
no one now; look away.

                   A stillness falls across the blue
ghetto of a life where it's been easy enough to lie down
freely with strangers, tower over them, leave them behind

for the other life, meaning this one, where a stillness falls
also, but this time the way shadows fall, weightless, and yet
they change everything, they change everything beneath them.

BLIZZARD

After agony had left his body to find another,
or in search of no one, just agony on its
own for once, merely cruising,
something stayed, like

       a precipitate—*grief, maybe,*
that's what they said,
as if such had ever been
grief's properties . . . Why is lying
to others always so much harder
than to ourselves? Yesterday, for example,
starlings in flight, the ice of
the frozen pond beneath them briefly
containing their shadows—not

           reflecting them,
not the way water does, the way
the water did, the way it will
in spring when the pond has unlocked itself
all over again with
no more regard than disregard

for the wings and faces that pass, or don't,
across it, so what,

                so what? When I say
I trust you, I mean I've considered
that you could betray me, which means I know
you will, that we'll have between us at last
that understanding which is a safer thing
than trust, not a worse,
not a better thing . . . Wanderer,
whisperer,
little firework, little

                  not-my-own, soon enough
the non-world we've been steering for
from the start: colorless, stripped of motion, all those
pleasures you knew so well how to give to others
gone also—pleasure,
I can hear you say, what world
was that

INTERIOR: ALL THE LEAVES
SHAKE OFF THEIR LIGHT

It was then we found ourselves too many fields away from
where we'd meant to be, with regard to desire, to get there
ever, even if—though this was not the case—we'd been
told the way. Sure, we'd developed a patience, perhaps
even a taste for being lost, but we were plain exhausted: not
in our bodies, which had forgotten nothing of what they'd

known of heat, or of what to do with it—wasn't it this that
had rescued us, mostly, from many worse persuasions, as we
passed the time?—but if not in our bodies, then where, where
else exhausted? *Come weather, come whatever-we've-sworn,*
we leave our tracks in the dirt where of course we have to,
say the ghosts in the walls, slurring their usual handful of notes

remembered of the song that, together, each touch, each bruise
equals. Then they fade like smoke, or a bit like regret. Who

cares, anymore, about ghosts? Our ambitions were very high; on occasion, we fell from them—swiftly, without surprise, and very far. Never, though, never would we have called that failure, no—not then, and not now either. For here we are.

IN THIS WORLD TO BE LOST

Get dressed—

     We should leave, now.

As for the so-called waters of persuasion,
why not cast what's left of belief
upon them?

     As when we come to love a thing
for no better reason than that we have found it,
and find it wants for love. Have you ever
done that?

     Some asleep-looking bird, say, that's
dead really, lying
dead in the straw-grass, the grass and
the imaginary conversation it makes
with itself . . .

Or any man in tears, whispering *If*
I go down on whoever tells me to, is it prayer,
isn't it, did I pray

enough?

Waves,
then waves in reverse—

                maybe that's all we're given.
Maybe stamina's just a fairer form of stubborn,
and maybe not. As for autumn,

that predictable drama will soon enough,
presumably,

            be again beginning. —Get dressed. And,
upon the confusion/unconfusion
that the waves make, let's cast what's left.

BOW, AND ARROW

Not the war, but the part just after,
when a great stillness whose beauty we'd have
missed, possibly, had we instead
been spared, hovers over the ruins.

★

Put your head in among the flowers—
do it: but for
me this time, not yourself, is what I think he said.

AS FOR THAT PIECE
OF SUNDOWN YOU'VE
BEEN WANTING

Like little forges for which the heart too often
gets mistaken, the dogs run ahead of me, just
out of earshot, across what's a field, and then
a coast: some stones, some sand. Funny how
sorrow more often arrives before honesty, than
the other way round. To my left, a blackness

like the past, but without the past's precision;
to my right, the ocean . . . Not so lost as I'd
been thinking, then—or had once, admittedly,
maybe even hoped for. Kingdom of what's left,
still, to be angry at, or forgive. All of the bees
flying at last out of me. We're traveling north.

UNDO IT

Deep from within the changing colors of a life
that itself keeps changing, I know the leaves prove
nothing—though it
                        does seem otherwise—about
how helplessness is not a luxury, not a hurt by
now worth all the struggling to take back, but
instead what we each, inevitably, stumble
sometimes into,

                        and sometimes through . . . As for
that grove-within-a-grove that desire has, so long,
looked like—*falling, proof of nothing*, carrion birds
clouding the slumped boughs of the mountain ash—

I can almost see again: we'll drown anyway—why not
in color? You're no more to me a mystery, than I to you.

LATE IN THE LONG APPRENTICESHIP

At last, he's asleep.
I can look at him the way I'm meant to.

His body moves like any ocean. The ocean moves like any field
back home: submission, submission's shadow, wind, submission.

SNOW GLOBE

Whatever falls is a thing descending. But
descent doesn't have to mean to fall. About nostalgia, I am
still against it. By morning, there was no evidence
of what had happened between us, or
not happened. How everything depends. The sound of bees
beginning to stir a last time all over again
in the walls of a house left wintering. A little
wind through the pines in stereo, making the limbs
stiffly rise, like memorials, for
those who choose to remember what's over in that
particular way, though I've never chosen it, and
do not now. My requirements, they're
what they've always been: a name I can use when riding
shotgun; then there's my secret name. I'm not the man I knew.

And now the rain in soft strokes coming down,
seeming to whisper of deaths that
weren't that heavenly after all, of lives cracked
open first, gutted—some of us fuck and call it
making love, for some it's the other way round—then
cast aside. *You could do worse, and probably will,*
he says to me, I say to him, he says, and
I say back. Even if the skitter of leaves in autumn
can be called proverbial—if I'm not,
for example, the man I knew—it is no less real,
any of it. Otherwise, what history have I got, with
which to shadow us in context, lost
ponies in a storm that's blinding, blinding. It blinds us both.

III

I keep waiting for change,

as opposed to the sign for change where it's occurred

already and I'm again too late. I keep

pretending it makes no difference when the moon

goes that do-what-you-must shade of red that there's

no real name for. As for how it feels, or

can sometimes: like a life, like life

itself, descending—sand cherry, chestnut, river birch,

dogwood, pear . . . All night, I ride shotgun side

by side with the ghost I call failure, for whom gesture, if

not entirely the one language left, is the only one

he still trusts, though there are times,

even now, I forget this: he takes my hand, and I hold it—

tight. And I turn my face away.

IV

Stumbling by moonlight upon your shadow-self—that
man you knew, or thought you did—see if he
stirs, first. Is he dead, or close to? If so, you could do
worse than to stroke him as you would the brow
of a broken pony, brushing away the flies that
you choose to call, instead, bees as they ascend and hover
slightly above the open wound, its
red business . . . Why should your requirements change
from what they've always been? Stay as blind as
ever to the particular form of failure that is
still nostalgia. Turn his face away. Let memory be
the only piece of evidence that you hold on to. Not leaves,
but—what is no less real—the ghosts of leaves. Do
what you must, but softly, soft as rain just beginning to turn to snow
at the cusp of winter. —Don't worry. This too is love.

BORDER SONG

If you're going to sing tonight,
why not a border song? How maybe there
is, in fact, a sorrow that even magic comes with,
how—never mind the catalpa coming meanwhile
back into white, believable, indifferent blossom—
you're still afraid; you'll always be . . .

But no stolen hours, for once, no
shuddering forms lifting themselves slowly up,
like memory, with its knack for breaking off again
to where remembering seems not remembering, but
dream, an easy one—a little restlessness,
then nothing. Just a border song.

BRONZE WHERE ONCE
THE BLUE HAD BEEN

Never entirely gone from me, he patrols the dark shore
of himself, it seems—shore to which
by now defeats, victories, come as seasonal
as foliage,

        and fade the same. His eyes
are wolf-eyes: tundra; storm; things that don't
belong here. *What's so wrong about knowing form
through touch,*

        not sight, he asks, like the latest
good drug, taking hold, and there are nights
I believe him. Want to. He's the difference between grace
and what simply happens because it does,

                not because
it must. I can tell the difference, by the way my telling it
each time keeps missing: not the stars, exactly,

and not their stillness,

                        or the shine of that, not the stranded
pail of stolen water where I can sometimes
almost forget to look for them, though
they have been there, glittering, relentless, all along.

BRACE OF ANTLERS

—Abbreviation for the animal's head, its body

—They say despair is belief's true echo

—I've seen how the sky becomes the echo of what's flown through it

48

SHIMMER

He'd have drowned, without me. The eyes
stay shut. The mouth spills
                                      slightly open. The lips
move, or the snow's movement makes them
seem to, I can't tell. The gulls huddle as they
will, in a storm, the snow
                                not so much settling on
as hovering about them, the wind in sudden gusts
lifting their feathers,
                                then the feathers finding again
those positions that make flight, for a time, look
possible. When did souvenirs of what happened start
becoming tokens of what
                                could have been becomes
one of those questions that, more and more, I keep
forgetting to stop asking. Now the snow seems a minor
chord; now a form of mercy—making
                                less hard the edges
of what's hard. What's the point, in asking?
Why not rest my head upon the mirror that his chest is?

YOUR BODY DOWN IN GOLD

You can make of the world's parts something
elemental, you can say the elements mean
something still worth fucking a way forward for:
maybe the dream coming true; maybe the dream,
true to form, coming undone all over again—
you can do that, or not, while a sail unfurls,
or a door

        blows shut . . . So it turns out there's more
of a difference between love and deep affection
than you'd have chosen. So what? Remember
the days of waking to disasters various, and of
at least in part your own doing, and saying
aloud to no one *I have decided how I would
like to live my life, and it isn't*

                this way, and
how you actually believed it: you'd change,
the world would? Man with a mourning dove in
one eye, rough seas in the other, lately the light—
more than usual, it seems—finds us brokenly. I say
let's brokenly start shouldering the light right back.

50

ANYONE WHO HAD A HEART

I know a man who routinely asks
that I humiliate him. It's sex, and it isn't—
whatever. For him, it's a need, the way
brutality can seem for so long a likely
answer, that

        it becomes the answer—
a kindness, even, and I have always
been kind, for which reason it goes
against my nature to do what he says, but
there's little in nature that won't, with
enough training, change . . .

              After it's done,
if the weather's good, we tour his garden:
heliotrope, evening primrose . . . *Proximity's
one thing*, he likes to say, *penetration
another*, and I have learned that's true,
though which is better depends: whose life?
what story? the relief

          of snowmelt,
or the flooded fields again? We go down

to the stables to visit the horses that,
when they were nothing, just shivering
foals still, he once asked me to give
names to. How long we've traveled,
he and I—more like

                drifted, really—and
how far. More black than all the sorrows
and joys put together that I can remember
when I try remembering, which I mostly don't,
now the foals,

                they're stallions. Call out
Fanfare, Adoration. Like broken kings,
they lower their heads, then raise them.

NOW YOU MUST GO
WHEREVER YOU WISH

In moments like this, when he shows what appears to be a purely
accidental grace, it seems
almost believable: death has changed him.

See how,
            as if having muscled finally a way clear of the dark,
a dark stripped of the very stars without which the night sky's
distance—and with it, the crossing of distance, meaning hope, risk,
ambition—wouldn't even be knowable,

                        he steps into the light, then out of it?

DOMINION

Sometimes I take the leather hood off—I
refuse to wear it. As if I were king. Or a man
who's free. Ravens, red-tailed hawks, the usual
flocks of drifting-most-of-the-time strangers
settle the way even things that drift

                  have to, and
I don't care. All over again, I know things that
nobody knows, or wants to—things that, though
prettier, maybe, against the snow

                  of memory, can
still hurt, all the same. Any blame falling where
it falls—that random. That moment each day
when the light traveling across what's always been
mine to at any point take back, or give elsewhere,
becomes just the light again, turning back to dark,
when the branches

                  stir as they've stirred forever,
more tenderly over some of us than others. Sing,
or don't sing. Help me take this leather hood off—
I refuse to wear it. I'm the king. I'm free.

BUT WAVES, THEY SCATTER

From beneath the ice field, longing looks up at the lovers
who—variously meandering, stalling or not, fucking
or not—guess nothing of him. Torturer sometimes. Known
also to have been a savior eventually, hard passage to a life
worth the hardness. You would think longing lived in a space
warmer than an ice field, you would think so. Tragedies are
happening everywhere in the world, beside things that aren't
technically tragedies, though they include suffering, pain, death
in its more humiliating versions, to remind that some of us
will be less spared, and some will not. Up through the ice field,
longing watches the lovers who, in turn, look down, or away,
laughing. Each time, they miss the ice field for the flowers that,
despite the cold, somehow grow there: distraction's the bluer
and more abundant flower, black at the edges. Joy is the other.

SILVERCHEST

Unafraid is what we were, I think, and then afraid,
though it mostly seemed otherwise. I opened my eyes,
I saw, I closed, I shut them.

                            The usual morning glories
twist up through banks of gone-wild-by-now holly;
crickets for song, morphos for their glamour, which
is quiet—blue, and quiet . . .

You: the dark that nothing, not even the light, displaces.
You, who have been the single leaf that
won't stop tossing,
among the others.
For you.

ACKNOWLEDGMENTS

Thank you to the editors of the following journals, in which these poems—some in different versions—originally appeared:

American Literary Review: "Distraction," "Shimmer"

Callaloo: "Black Swan on Water, in a Little Rain," "Snow Globe"

Cerise Press: "Bow, and Arrow"

The Chronicle of Higher Education Arts & Academe blog: "My Meadow, My Twilight"

Connotation Press: An Online Artifact: "As for That Piece of Sundown You've Been Wanting"

Fence: "Flight of Doves"

Granta: "Undo It"

Green Mountains Review: "And Other Animals," "Bluegrass," "Bronze Where Once the Blue Had Been," "Dominion"

The Harvard Advocate: "The Jetty," "Anyone Who Had a Heart"

The Journal: "The Difference Between Power and Force"

The Kenyon Review: "In This World to Be Lost"

New England Review: "So the Mind Like a Gate
Swings Open," "Blizzard," "Border Song,"
"Now You Must Go Wherever You Wish"

The New Republic: "But Waves, They Scatter"

The New York Times: "Interior: All the
Leaves Shake Off Their Light"

Provincetown Arts: "Now Rough, Now Gentle"

Quarterly West: "Neon"

Salt Hill: "First You Must Cover Your Face"

Slate: "Silverchest"

Smartish Pace: "Late in the Long Apprenticeship"

The Southampton Review: "After the Afterlife,"
"Darkness Is As Darkness Does"

The Southern Quarterly Review: "Ghost Hour"

Sugar House Review: "Your Body Down in Gold"

West Branch: "Surrounded As We Are, Unlit, Unshadowed"

Willow Springs: "Just the Wind for a Sound,
Softly" (as "And It Begins Like This")

★

The epigraph is Carolyn Kizer's translation, from her book *Knock Upon
Silence* (Garden City, NY: Doubleday & Company, 1965).

"Just the Wind for a Sound, Softly": the sentence "It is hard to see anyone who has become like your own body to you" is from Willa Cather's short story "Neighbour Rosicky."

"Distraction": the image referred to occurs early in book VIII of Virgil's *Aeneid*.

"Blizzard": the last ten lines are my translation of and variation on the poem "Animula, Vagula, Blandula," attributed to the Roman emperor Hadrian. My version originally appeared as its own poem in *Great River Review*.

"In This World to Be Lost": the title is from a sentence in Thoreau's *Walden*, "not till we are completely lost, or turned round—for a man needs only to be turned round once with his eyes shut in this world to be lost—do we appreciate the vastness and strangeness of nature."

"Anyone Who Had a Heart" is also the title of a song by Burt Bacharach and Hal David.

"Now You Must Go Wherever You Wish": the title is the last line of John N. Morris's poem "After the Closing," from *Selected Poems* (St. Louis: The Press at Washington University, 2002).

61